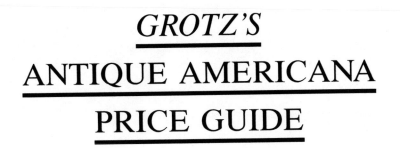

GROTZ'S
ANTIQUE AMERICANA
PRICE GUIDE

Also by George Grotz

FROM GUNK TO GLOW

THE FURNITURE DOCTOR

THE NEW ANTIQUES

ANTIQUES YOU CAN DECORATE WITH

INSTANT FURNITURE REFINISHING

STAINING AND REFINISHING UNFINISHED FURNITURE
   AND OTHER NAKED WOODS

DECORATING FURNITURE WITH A LITTLE BIT OF CLASS

THE ANTIQUE RESTORER'S HANDBOOK

THE CURRENT ANTIQUE FURNITURE STYLE AND PRICE GUIDE

THE FUN OF REFINISHING FURNITURE

GROTZ'S 2ND ANTIQUE FURNITURE STYLE AND PRICE GUIDE

GROTZ'S DECORATIVE COLLECTIBLES PRICE GUIDE

DOUBLE YOUR MONEY IN ANTIQUES IN 60 DAYS

GROTZ'S

ANTIQUE AMERICANA

PRICE GUIDE

by GEORGE GROTZ

DOUBLEDAY & COMPANY, INC.
GARDEN CITY, NEW YORK
1987

Library of Congress Cataloging-in-Publication Data
The Antique Americana price guide.

   Title on added t.p.: Grotz's antique Americana
price guide.

   1. Americana—Collectors and collecting—Catalogs.
I. Grotz, George.   II. Title: Grotz's antique Americana
price guide.
NK805.A76   1987   745.1'0973'075   86–16517
ISBN 0-385-19514-1

ACKNOWLEDGMENTS

For the use of photographs and/or information we would like to thank the following for their gracious help and cooperation:

Bonner's Barn, Malone, New York, a leading dealer in Americana; the auction house of Richard A. Bourne, Hyannis Port, Massachusetts; Garth Auctions, Inc., Delaware, Ohio; Leonard's Antiques, Seekonk, Massachusetts.

CONTENTS

Preface
ANTIQUES ON THE GO
THE CURRENT BOOM IN AMERICANA

Only in the last ten years has attention been paid to antiques for their distinctly American character—especially to folk art and primitive pieces. As a result, the value of such objects has risen sharply.

For instance, country-made chairs in imitation of English styles—"Country Chippendale"—have quadrupled in price in the five years since I reported them to be severely undervalued in my first price guide—*The Current Antique Furniture Style and Price Guide.*

All of the objects shown in this book will certainly rise faster than the standard lines of English and French antiques, based simply on the momentum of the current interest in Americana. But especially sharp rises may be expected in anything antique that can be fitted behind the seats of an expensive sports car and hung on the wall of a stockbroker's condominium. In other words, objects that will appeal to the newly rich of the Reagan era of prosperity.

One category of antiques that fills the bill for this demand is folk art of all kinds. Especially hand-carved and painted wooden figures.

Early paintings and prints will continue to rise at a faster pace than the rest of the categories.

Early photographic prints and cameras are already zooming.

Antique toys, dolls, and Teddy bears also fill the bill.

What this means is that while antique furniture will always be as sound an investment as you can make, it will not be one of the leading categories in the current bull market in antiques. Nor can anything spectacular be expected in pewter, China, earthenware, stoneware, clocks, or fabrics such as quilts—the standard categories.

(Incidentally, furniture that has been false-grained or otherwise decorated with paint comes under "folk art"—not simply "furniture.")

As my friend Sam Pennington always says, "The rich people of tomorrow are investing in antiques today. The problem is knowing which ones." Well, here's a price guide that accurately reflects today's collecting interests. I think you will find it to be a useful companion book to *Double Your Money in Antiques in 60 Days,* my other current book that is selling like hotcakes in your friendly neighborhood bookstore. (Advt.)

—**George Grotz**

GROTZ'S
ANTIQUE AMERICANA
PRICE GUIDE

Andirons

Pair of brass steeple andirons from New York City, circa 1775. Twenty inches tall.
$450.

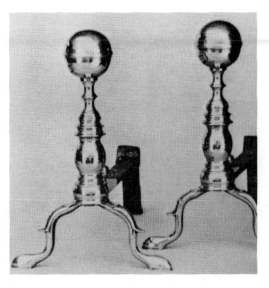

Pair of brass ball-top andirons by Hunneman, circa 1815, in perfect condition.
$525.

Early steeple-top bell-metal andirons with maker's initials on firedogs. Seventeen inches high.
$750.

Victorian urn-topped andirons, circa 1900. Nice brass and iron, but only **$150.**

Hand-wrought iron andirons with ring top from almost any year in the 1700s.
$225.

These brass andirons in unrestored condition are covered with caked soot, but are still in the **$450** area.

Baskets

Swing-handle egg basket. Mound rises in the center of the bottom. Very fine workmanship of oak handle and frame makes collectors bid high on these; retail value is about **$350.**

A very popular potato basket from northern New England. Age can only be guessed as they were made the same way from 1830 to 1950. Made of ash, very sturdy. Hard to find with cover. About three feet high.
$165.

Corn or wheat basket for carrying either to the mill to be ground. Late 1800s. Oak handle and woven ash splints.
$125.

Swing-handle basket of ash splints
with handle and top loops made of
oak. Late 1800s. Used for gathering
eggs or apples, a very handy basket.
Most were broken from hard use, so
survivors go for
$250.

Sewing basket with cover—maybe
1920s—used for storing sewing
materials. Dyed splints are of the
kind used for chair seats—ash,
hickory, or elm. Only about 14
inches in diameter.
$50.

Farm utility basket from the late
1800s. Made of ash and oak with
very nice woodwork that makes it
worth around
$220.

Weathered elm-splint utility farm basket from early 1900s, often called a butter basket, worth around **$80.**

Covered lunch basket from around 1910. Handmade of fine ash splint, but on a production line. **$60.**

A picking basket made in 1915. The side with two handles was hung on the side of a wagon owned by a berry-picking family that supplemented its farm income by picking other people's berries in the spring. Worth **$120.**

5

Beds

Cannonball four-posters were common for over a century, but this one has fancy acanthus leaf carving on bell under ball and is made of tiger and bird's-eye maple. Height 47 inches. Value,
$1,800.

Sheraton birch tester bed with fluted footposts. Reduced to single-bed size for modern mattresses.
$1,450.

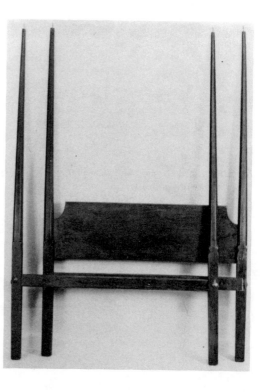

Pencil-post bed with original soft-blue paint. Also such pure proportions.
$1,200.

Low-post Empire bed, circa 1840, with fine bold turnings and tiger maple panels in headboard. Original condition, **$1750.**

Sheraton tester bed of maple with fluted swelling columns, circa 1800. Refinished, **$1,800.**

Deeply turned ball-and-ring bed with "rolling pin" headboard. Note hand-planing marks on headboard, which has been raised to accommodate standard mattress. Pegs on top of lower frame were to hold original rope mattress. Maple turnings with pine headboard, stained by original maker to look like mahogany. **$800.**

Cannonball four-poster in nice rose-colored grain-streaked paint. Made 1830. Blanket-roll turning across foot. Angle irons on frame hold modern mattress. Without paint: $700. With paint: **$1,200.**
("They buy the paint, Matilda!")

Exquisite "Shaker-type" maple-framed hired man's bed with pine headboard. A work of art for only **$750.**

Empire four-poster in rose-grain paint with cannonball-and-bell-post turnings. 1860s.
$950.

Three close-ups of turnings on simple rope beds from the middle 1700s. An example of how functionalism in design enables an unsophisticated craftsman to create pure poetry in wood. This is what Americana is all about!

High-low acorn-post bed with a
double tombstone headboard. 1810s,
which is early for this type of bed.
Pine headboard in maple frame.
$1,200.

Simple "Shaker-type" hired man's or
child's bed in pine and maple.
Design is at the heart of American
functionalism. But still only
$750.
(May be a great investment at that
price.)

10

Three papered hatboxes from same maker in New Hampshire, circa 1850.
$750.

Sealskin-covered box 14 inches long with original wallpaper lining and label of James Oldden of Philadelphia, lined with newspapers of 1875, hand decorated with green pine trees.
$125.

Dovetailed pine sea chest from around 1850. Excellent decoration, a popular and historically authentic object.
$650.

A nice old pine sea chest or clothes locker that was redecorated in the 1920s. If the dumb paint job were stripped off, it would be worth around
$150.

Wooden hatbox with original decoration. As high as
$300.

Shaker boxes, all by same maker, painted in various colors. From 3 to 14 inches in diameter.
$6,500.

Carved oak box 14 inches long made by early English settler in New England. Usually used for deeds or other valuable papers.
$450.

Pillar-and-scroll clock with brass finials by Seth Thomas, 27 inches high. Thirty-hour wooden-works movement. Reverse painting, dial, and inside labels in excellent condition. Maple and mahogany veneer. Plus or minus **$2,000.**

Federal weight-driven pendulum clock with thirty-hour movement. Excellent reverse glass painting on door, carved eagle on top. **$800.**

Seth Thomas of Connecticut rosewood-veneer shelf clock in excellent condition and maker's label intact inside. Brass eight-day time-and-strike movements. Still great accuracy when adjusted. **$400** range.

13

Fine Gilbert steeple clock with mahogany veneer on pine case, eight-day movement and chimes. Two steeples are in the $300 range, four steeples as high as **$650.**

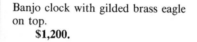

Banjo clock with gilded brass eagle on top.
$1,200.

Carved column clock from Connecticut, circa 1830. Thirty-hour time-and-strike movement run by weights.
$700.

14

Empire shelf clock from the mid-1800s of mahogany veneer on pine. Brass works and hourly chime driven by separate spring for almost a week. $150. With rosewood veneer, close to
$200.

All brass, exposed-works solid brass clock that hangs on the wall. Release movement driven by weights (not shown). As is,
$650.

Fascinating carnival watch given as a prize. Hung on the back wall of a booth, it looked real. When you win it, all you get is a real case with a piece of paper on which the face and hands are printed. Well, I like it:
$10.

Carnival watch opened.

Alarm clock from the 1920s with a French or Tiffany style about it. Gold plated.
$125.

A handyman's special of mahogany veneer on pine. About $70 as shown. Stripped of the veneer and turned into Early American pine, an amazing
$220.

Very stylish 1920s case clock in a block of lucite. This is not Art Deco —though usually called that. It is really a result of the French influence on the period. So I hereby name this sort of thing "The Scott Fitzgerald Style."
$225.

Tall case clock derivative of the English style but made in the colonies in the early 1700s. Simplification is the American design element. Also semimass production.
$1,800.

Tall clock, circa 1800, from New Jersey or Pennsylvania. Made of cherry with hand-cut brass works by William Randall. Dial is brass with engraved angels.
$4,500 area.

Pennsylvania inlaid-walnut tall clock made in late 1700s. Phases-of-the-moon picturegraph over face. Fine condition.
$3,800.

Waltham pocket watch with unusually large numbers and a solid gold case. The big numbers made them handy for engineers, who could see them even in the dark cabs of their locomotives. The gold case drives its worth up to
$650.

Waltham railroad watch for conductors and engineers.
$850.

Back of a "railroad" watch.

Clock of white metal (a hard lead) with vines for legs, circa 1915. This is an example of Art Nouveau that was made widely for the masses, in imitation of the Tiffany style. Brass works from the New Haven Clock Company still work. About one foot high.
$175.

Big Ben alarm clock from the 1920s with either black or white face and nickel-plated body.
$85.

Very Art Deco alarm clock.
$125.

Empire ogee-curve case clock of
figured mahogany on pine.
Pendulum-regulated movement.
$250 to **$300.**

A "figure-eight" schoolhouse wall
clock made in Connecticut by
E. Ingraham & Company with time
only eight-day movement. Brass
pendulum and original label.
$550.

Solid brass sundial with face
engraved with roman numerals.
Corner broken and attached to board
with new screws. As is, $125. Good
ones up to
$500.

Child's ladder-back high chair from 1700s. Maple and ash with original old dark-red blood-and-milk paint. **$650** to **$700.**

Shaker-type armchair with cookie turnings on tops of front legs. An armchair usually painted in black and bearing factory number is really Shaker, in which case the price is **$650.**

Pennsylvania ladder-back chair of
common variety.
$175.

Typical ladder-back chair with
sausage turnings on back posts, circa
1760s, usually made out of maple
with reed seat, ash slats. Old red
paint finish, authentically worn.
$650.

22

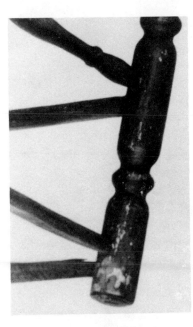

Three close-up photos of the turnings details on some of the preceding chairs. As these 1700s chairs were often used on dirt floors of log cabins, the bottom of the legs often rotted. The erosion process has taken 3 inches off the bottom of the legs on this chair.

Cookie top on front leg of armchair.

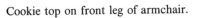

Sweet finial of maple.

Shaker armchair rocker made in Factory No. 6 with cookie-ended arms and carpet-cutter rockers, all original except for new braided seat and back.
$400.
Better turnings on tops of posts and larger cookies . . .

. . . as seen in this stripped frame, would push the price up to around **$850.**

Rush-seated chairs showing curves of Sheraton influence, from the late 1800s. With new seats, **$85** each.

Shaker armchair with accurately
reproduced webbing seat and back
from Ohio.
$650.

Bentwood Shaker rocker of late
1800s. Cloth webbing seat and back
are accurate replacements.
$450.

Typical "Country Chippendale" side
chair made in the winter by a
country carpenter in the mid-1700s.
Maple and cherry were the common
woods used. This one has a new
rush seat. Up to $600 and still
rising.

Early chair by country cabinetmaker
has a Chippendale back and Queen
Anne legs, slip seat. In fine
condition, made of cherry wood.
$1,400.

Queen Anne all-American-made
chair in cherry wood, from the early
1700s: A true gem of craftsmanship
and style. A really great object.
$1,600.

A cherry Queen Anne corner chair
—even though side and back legs are
Marlborough, as in Chippendale.
This chair dates from the late 1700s.
A quality piece in the
$1,200 range.

Rare, country-made chair with design elements of William and Mary. From the early eighteenth century.
$1,100.

Bannister-back side chair with unusual molded front surface of vertical bannisters. Also unusual turnings on back posts.
$450.

Pair of transitional Queen-Anne-to-Chippendale chairs with rush seats to show that they are an American variation. American country-mades.
$750 the pair.

Bannister-back chair from 1740 with a Victorian seat cushion put on it about 1880. Also painted in the middle 1800s.
$475.

Corner chair with old splint seat of ash still in perfect condition. Mahogany legs and hickory back. Circa 1750. The real thing.
$1,600.

Cage-back Windsor side chair with bamboo turnings. Top of the line—a masterpiece for only
$550.

Fan-backed Windsor chair with very splayed legs and nicely curved lines to seat. Bamboo-turned legs from 1780s.
$750.

On this fan-backed Windsor chair, the fan has been braced with iron rods and the rockers have been added, so collectors will only have to pay in the $500 range. Whereas, a perfect edition of this chair might go for
$1,500.

Windsor child's high chair with sausage turned legs and nice chunky seat to hold the four leg-tops securely. From 1770.
$1,400.

29

Set of four thumb-back or rabbit-ear chairs. These are Windsors because the legs go right into thick pine seat, as opposed to there being a frame beneath the seat. Now called Kitchen Windsors. For the set of four,
$1,800.

Rod-backed Windsor rocking chair with set-back arms to accommodate hoop skirts. Early 1800s.
$550.

Desk armchair with drawer from the 1850s. Thick pine seat and back. Usually called a "Captain's" chair, but really is simply a writing chair for a student or clerk.
$280.

30

Side chair with added rockers.
$75.

Pennsylvania rocker in original green
paint, scroll seat and stenciled
decoration, circa 1840.
$350.

Boston rocker in original paint and
worn decoration, circa 1830. Lots of
them around.
$325.

Arrow-backed pine-and-maple rocker with writing arm from western Massachusetts, circa 1840.
$575.

Arrow-backed bench from the late 1800s showing the Windsor principle of mounting all the legs and spokes in a thick plank seat. A cousin of the Boston and Salem rockers of the same period. Pine arms and seat, the rest maple.
$475.

Strangely low-backed fan-back Windsor with nice splay to legs from 1790s.
$375.

Clumsy Windsor chair from late
1800s called a firehouse Windsor.
$275.

This continuous-back Windsor
armchair with extra braces at back is
unrestored, has traces of original
black paint and is in the
$2,500 and up range.

A fine 1920s reproduction by
Wallace Nutting of a Windsor fan-
backed side chair has a rarity about
it that makes it worth as much as an
authentic antique—which is
$900.

33

Seven-spindle bow-back Windsor side chair from New Hampshire with slightly worn-off legs is still in the $400-plus class.

Windsor bow-back armchair has deep saddle seat, knuckles at end of arms. Traces of original paint. Top of the line at $3,000 plus.

Pennsylvania fiddle-back Windsor chair with original decoration, fine scroll seat. From the 1850s. $165.

Fiddle-back settee of maple with pine seat, fine carved arms and Windsor legs.
$625.

Uncomfortable swayback is feature of this Pennsylvania Windsor rocker which still has original paint.
$375.

Victorian country "cracker-barrel" chairs found in country stores and offices. Made entirely of oak.
$125 each.

Set of six matching Hitchcock
chairs, redecorated, reglued and
newly caned. Still strong and useful.
Around
    $2,000.

American Sheraton-style ladies'
fancy chair or bedroom chair. This
chair has a rush seat and was once
originally painted. From the 1830s.
Flimsy things, which may be why
they bring only
    $150.

Set of four Empire-related fiddle-
back chairs with cane seats and
original black streaks of paint on
red-dyed wood. $200 each,
    $800 for the set.

Vase splat-back chair of imitation rosewood (black streaks on red) from late 1800s. Around **$75.**

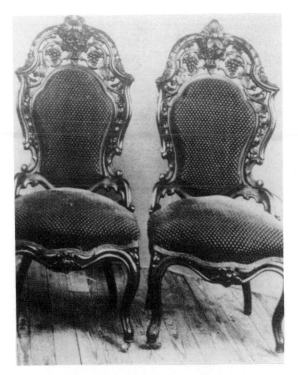

Real Belter chairs, i.e., made in New York City by John Belter's furniture shop in the late 1800s. At least **$4,500** for the pair.

Walnut Eastlake chairs with the original uncomfortable horsehair upholstery still on them. Made in the 1890s. You can get all three for only $400 on the East Coast, $600 in the Midwest or $1,200 in Los Angeles from one of those movie producers.

Whatever else they may have been, Americans of the Victorian era were certainly eclectic. And this chair is a good example. It has a Gothic back, Louis XVI legs and a big, wide Eastlake seat. And that's American! Solid walnut. Interesting, maybe, but not sought after.
$150.

Victorian Renaissance style inspired by Italian version of Louis XV, which I realize is pretty involved, and which it is pretty nervy to then classify as Americana. But it is something Americans did make, and it is part of American culture of the 1860s. Anyway,
$650.

Late Victorian Belter-style side chairs. Backs are made out of laminated rosewood to give them strength; intricately carved. Left, **$1,100.** Right,
$1,400.

38

Hard-to-find, simple, Chippendale-inspired stool in cherry with old varnish stain, circa 1760.
$750.

An authentic Chippendale wing chair with the square Marlborough legs. Even though they always have to be reupholstered, the small ones go at auction for up to $2,500, the big ones for almost twice that. A certain cachet might reflect on the owner of an antique of which only 10 percent can be seen.

Bucket bench sat on the sunny side of the house to keep the water in the buckets warm all day. Pine, decorated with sponged-on pattern.
$350.

Pew bench made of heavy pine boards, from the late 1700s.
$350.

Chests

Bonnet-top highboy in the Queen Anne manner with nice carved fans. Circa 1750. American, of course, because it is done in maple. All English ones were in mahogany. Top of the line—
$25,000 and up.

Pennsylvania walnut chest on frame with nicely carved Chippendale ball, claw feet and delicate apron. Original brasses.
$3,200.

Flat-topped Queen Anne highboy from New England, circa 1750. Made of maple. Has its original hand-struck brasses, and is top of the line. Easily $15,000 at auction. And $25,000 on any millionaire's row.

Chippendale chest-on-chest in dark American walnut. Characteristic dentil molding on top, original brasses, mint condition. But dating from the 1800s, so only around **$4,500.**

Five graded drawers of tiger maple on this early 1700s chest. Drawers are top of the line, so this goes for **$5,500.**

Swell-front bureau with brass knobs that is a cross between the Sheraton (front posts) and Empire styles. Made circa 1815. Pineapples on tops of front columns very desirable. A very American piece. Mahogany veneer.
$1,800.

Dunlap highboy with ball-and-claw feet, circa 1780. Made in New Hampshire. This piece made of cherry wood, with its *original finish* and "architectural" top, is a collector's item suitable for museums. This is it.
$40,000.

All-maple chest-on-chest. Date unknown, made by unknown country cabinetmaker, but still
$5,500.

Simple Empire chest of drawers, circa 1830, still retains Sheraton front columns.
$400.

Authentic highboy base with new
piece of wood put on the top to
make it into a sideboard.
$2,250.

Early American lowboy in the
Queen Anne manner with boldly
curved legs and deeply carved fan.
Cherry wood.
$3,750.

American-made version of an
English Hepplewhite sideboard with
too-strong spade feet, from the mid-
1800s. Side cupboards have fake
drawer fronts. Figured mahogany
veneer.
$1,200.

43

Cherry four-drawer Sheraton chest that was originally stained to look like darker red mahogany. Beehive posts. Not a popular style—
$450.

Chippendale ogee curved feet on frame supporting mahogany chest. With reproduction Chippendale brass pulls instead of these Empire knobs (ugly!) it should bring
$4,200.

Five-drawer oak bachelor's chest, circa 1890. In the country: $150. In New York City or Chicago: $350. In Atlanta: $75. New Orleans: $25. Los Angeles: $450. Dallas: not saleable. (It's an interesting world out there in the antiques business!)

Flashy Empire chest with flame mahogany veneer over pine on drawer fronts, circa 1840. Because of the amazing veneer: $1,200. With ordinary figureless veneer:
$250.

All-pine blanket chest with original milk-blood paint and original brasses. Top lifts. Two top drawers are false. Two bottom drawers do not pull out.
$1,500!

Pine chest of drawers made in 1750. Missing all brasses and in need of artistic touching up of the original milk-blood paint.
$1,200.

Tiger maple drawers make this Sheraton chest with Empire knobs worth
$1,500.
(In mahogany, it would be worth only $325.)

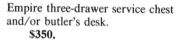

Empire three-drawer service chest and/or butler's desk.
$350.

Pennsylvania version of Chippendale four-drawer chest in cherry with original brass.
$1,950.

American Hepplewhite chest from
the early 1700s, maybe 1730s,
decorated with a feather in a stylized
way to imitate grain of Honduras
mahogany. It is actually pine, and
such early false-grained painted
pieces are rare. So,
$5,500.

Six-drawer chest from middle 1700s
that was painted in the late 1800s.
An antique dealer's "find" for
restoration. As is: $1,400. Restored:
$3,500.

A cherry Pennsylvania chest of
drawers with paneled sides that date
it circa 1850. A very nice piece of
furniture for only
$350.

Classic oak man's chest of drawers
in the "golden oak" style, dating
from the 1900s.
$175
out in the real world. Double and
more in the big cities.

Pennsylvania cupboard made in the
1850s. This piece has an expansion
top that opens up and then twists
around so that the leaves are
supported by the ends of the case. It
is made of tulip poplar, and is
unusual because it hasn't been
stained cherry, as poplar so often is.
$375.

Old apothecary chest with original
paint and base, circa 1770s. An
interior decorator's delight.
$1,800.

Lift-top blanket chest with nice molding used to simulate two top drawers. Pine with traces of old red milk-and-blood paint. Legs are cut out of solid-board sides. A classic piece at about $950. Hand-blown bell jars, circa 1850, **$175** each.

Two-drawer lift-top blanket chest from the 1820s. This still has the bold original paint and the original Sheraton knobs. As is, $1,200. Ones like this that have been stripped and refinished are only **$550.**

Exceptionally bold false graining in milk paint and Chippendale bracket feet make this pine lift-top blanket chest a real gem for collectors of primitive pieces. They buy the paint, as the saying goes, and this paint is in the $4,500 range. And going up.

This decorated and stenciled chest, which is only three feet long, was probably a seaman's chest before Sarah got it. Circa the 1820s; in pine, of course. In the $350–$400 range.

Small paneled Pennsylvania chest, circa 1830s. Old dull-brown paint in need of touch-up.
$450.

Blanket chest with bracket base, circa 1800. Stripped years ago.
$375.

50

Document or letter box with owner's
initials and original grain paint on it:
At shows: $250 to $275. Of course,
if your initials are "B.P." . . . well,
don't tell the dealer!

Early bible box with punch
decoration, mortised pine, circa
1750. At big-city antique shows they
amazingly sell for as much as
$750.

Pennsylvania lift-top chest with
excellent decoration and turnip feet.
With paint, $700. Refinished,
$350.

51

Paneled blanket chest with original ogee feet, circa 1780. Paneling is unusual this early.
$750.

Blanket box from late 1800s bearing odd decorations.
$175.

This special chest, circa the 1820s, was decorated with smoke from a candle while the paint was still wet. (It should be in a museum to preserve the decoration.) Worth from **$1,600** to **$1,800.**

Unusual Pennsylvania dower chest painted with two hearts sits on frame with strange little apron in center. The motif of this super decoration pushes value of this up to around
$1,500.

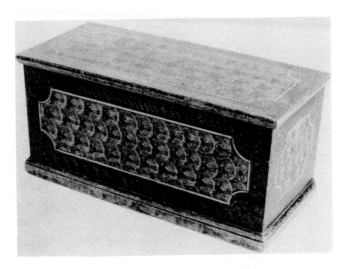

Decorated lift-top chest from 1830s. Not that old, but nice paint.
$550.

A two-foot-long dowry box from the last half of the eighteenth century. Note Greek-Federal look of design. As said before, they love the original paint.
$800.

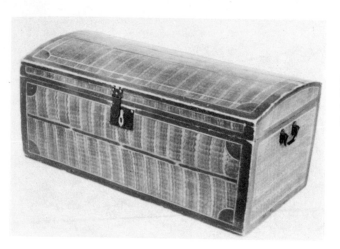

Grain-painted pine carriage box from late 1800s. Paint texture achieved with a feather. Because of the paint, $350. Stripped and refinished, only **$150.**

One-drawer blanket chest, circa 1825. Made in Pennsylvania out of tulip wood. Neither graceful nor delicate, but
$350.

Top: Brass-bound camphor chest brought back from China by whaling ship. Forty inches long.
$450.
Bottom: Six-board pine chest of the type whaling men took to sea. Original blue paint. Fifty-six inches long.
$175.

A ship's carpenter's chest from the
early 1800s. This chest is 38 inches
long, with decorated panels and
sliding trays and dividers.
  $375.

Couches

Federal loveseat with grapes and eagle-headed serpents. A really flamboyant piece even for the Federal style. With upholstery stripped and in need of refinishing, still $8,500. Totally restored, **$12,500.**

Federal couch in the 1820s manner of Duncan Phyfe. (Federal style is the distinctly American version of the Empire style of France that was decreed by Napoleon. Eagles, of course, are especially American.) $3,800 with original upholstery. Restored, **$8,500.**

A country-made, very primitive sofa
deriving from the Federal–Duncan
Phyfe–Empire conception, made out
of chunks of pine. A real collector's
item or museum piece. As is,
   $3,500.

This "reclining sofa" from the 1840s
is more Empire than Federal. Made
of mahogany. Restored this way,
$3,500. Piano stool,
   $450.

Cupboards

Pine corner cupboard from early 1800s. Glass is all old. Especially good lines for a piece that is all pine; therefore,
$2,600.

Corner cupboard with two doors from the first half of the 1800s. Very country-made, entirely of pine. Only
$1,800.

Pine country cupboard from the late 1800s with floating panels and replacement white porcelain knobs. **$850.**

Nicely finished cherry corner cupboard. This cupboard is from the early 1800s, but the original glass panes and dividers have been removed, Victorian hardware applied. Nevertheless, **$1,600.**

Fabulous tiger-maple cupboard in a design popular in Ohio and Illinois. Paneled doors indicate 1840s. Unusual base corners slant to front. Because of the terrific wood grain, **$3,600.**

Very Early American pewter cupboard filled with pewter, of course, made by country cabinetmaker in the 1760s. Nice primitive beaded edges to pine boards, solid-piece pine doors with turnbuckle that *looks* real, anyway. A good investment at $1,800 to the knowledgeable buyer.

Strange clothes press on top of chest of drawers (for very tall family?). This disturbing piece is late Victorian, circa the 1890s, but no identifiable style. Unrelated false graining probably applied as an afterthought.
$350.

Same cupboard, but close-up of pewter. Plates from $65 to $125. Small beakers, $65. Pitchers, tankards, and urns, $250 to $350. (All prices for unmarked pieces. Marked pieces would be double to five times as much depending on the rarity of the mark.)

Well-proportioned step-back cupboard with old glass in the doors, circa 1870s. Not very early, but nice. Needs stripping and refinishing, so $1,100 as is. Restored, **$1,800.**

With finely made drawers and all that old wood showing on the inside we have lots of the history of America for only $4,200. (Earlier and purer pieces like this, attributable to famous cabinetmakers, go for $25,000 and up.)

Cherry secretary with "blind doors." Classic bracket base is sort of Queen Anne; thin inlay strip around drawers from Hepplewhite; but in the end, all-American. See next photo.

Sheraton-into-Art-Deco sideboard with holes for wine bottles, made in the 1830s. Only $3,500, but what a buy for the speculator.

Late Pennsylvania dry sink for washing dishes, circa 1900. Made of poplar that will stain up to look like nice cherry.
$450.

Later corner cupboard from 1850s with lots of crackled paint over pine boards. Pennsylvania paneled doors and wavy glass. As is, $1,200. Refinished,
$2,000.

Small one-door pantry cupboard from late 1700s in old paint over pine. This piece has a raised panel in the door and sides.
$650.

Decoy step-back cupboard with excellent proportions, missing top door, very wide one on bottom. Probably only kitchen or cooking-shed cupboard, but talk about functionalism in design! An exceptional buy for the "discriminating collector" at only
$750.

A maple and pine desk-on-frame from the late 1700s with an assembly of pieces done in the Victorian era. But people will buy anything in dark brown wood, so this piece will bring **$650.**

63

Decoys

Hollowed-out folk decoy made by a farmer for his own use. Date unknown (and unimportant). Not greatly valued by decoy collectors but a fine piece of folk art. Sold as an object to be used as interior decoration, $175 to $225. Sold by a big-city dealer in folk art,
$750 to $1,200.

Land Brandt goose decoy for use on a mussel bed or marsh area. Date unknown. Handmade (note plane marks) but not folk art because it is one of many made by a decoy-maker. In original paint,
$400 to $500.

Crow decoy used by farmers to attract crows to the edge of a field where a farmer would be lurking in the bushes to shoot them. Black paint, of course. $175. Or, it could be a wood pigeon painted black to look like a crow—same price.

A Scaup duck decoy with golden eyes. Female, in original paint, nice form. A collector's item. Unsigned, $350. If signed,
$700.

Eagle from the 1860s, a patriotic symbol in the folk art category. Original paint in fine condition makes it worth in the area of
$1,800.

A fake decoy from Canada with the neck typically overdone. It is nicely painted, although crack in the body shows wood wasn't thoroughly cured. Since these are so popular, they sell for
$150.

A wood-duck decoy made by a professional decoy-maker for decoration—just to show as a work of art. Collectors of decoys will pay up to $800 for an unsigned one like this. Signed by famous decoy-makers they go into the thousands of dollars, depending on the name of the maker. A recent world-record price for one was $18,000. (Collectors of lots of things like this go crazy.)

Goose decoy in the "hisser" position. Made by some hunter-farmer, so it falls in the folk art class, but there are so many geese decoys around that this one would sell for only
$350.

Clockwise: Male Goldeneye duck
decoy, 1910, original paint, $500.
Primitive short-necked Canada goose
decoy, repainted, only $175. Factory-
made female Mallard, good paint,
$800. Mallard in original paint,
    $750.

Canadian rooster, a sort of modern
folk art from above the border. Well
decorated, they go for around $200.
If it were an antique one from
Pennsylvania, it would be worth
from
    $1,200 to $1,400.

This tugboat-bodied Canada goose
decoy is roughly shaped from a log.
Not a collectible decoy, but a
farmer's folk art object going
currently for around
    $400.

Merganser ducks like this one live in Canada but winter in our northern states. Homemade, repainted with a little sponged-on paint. Even so, they are very collectible.
$400.

Late 1800s Mallard duck with fine detail, once part of a sign. The quality and oddity put it in the **$1,800** class.

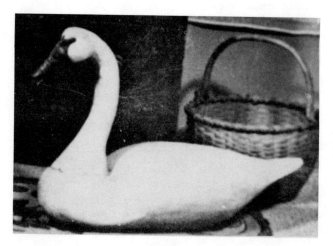

A really good swan decoy made by a professional decoy-maker around 1863. Original finish weathered just enough. Both decoy collectors and folk art people will pay $2,500 for this.

Desks

Slant-front New Hampshire desk in
the sought-after tiger maple.
Country-made simplification of the
Chippendale style.
   $4,500.

Sheraton–Empire–Queen Anne desk
from the late 1800s. An interesting
oddity for
   $650.

Primitive desk from the 1890s with nice slanted back. Only **$75.**

Fancy American-decorated Sheraton side or dressing table, or desk, with original stenciling that is in extraordinarily good condition. For decorations, **$1,800.**

Slant-top desk of tiger maple, circa 1770s. The real thing, and because of the wood, **$5,800.**

Tulipwood country-made writing
desk from Pennsylvania from the
1880s.
$750.

Lift-top country-made school desk.
Nice-looking old pine.
$85.

Simple American Sheraton dressing
table or desk, circa 1840s, made of
maple, pine, and mahogany.
$325.

Country schoolmaster's desk from the early 1800s. Made of pine with original dark red blood-and-milk paint varnished over.
$550.

Captain's desk with rolltop, flip lid from the 1840s. You keep it on a shelf and put it on a table to use it.
$450.

Fall-front desk top from the 1860s designed to be carried around and put on any table that would hold it.
$225.

Brass-bound writing or traveling desk in open position, fitted with ink bottle and candle holders (shown in place). This very fine example in perfect condition is in the **$500** range.

Schoolmaster's secretary-desk with blind doors on top, circa 1810. Hepplewhite-Sheraton in the American style of mixing English ones. The real thing, **$1,800.**

Maple slant-front desk with fan-in bottom drawer. Delicate frame with bib in center all add up to a 1770s New Hampshire American masterpiece for **$6,500.**

Rolltop desk with tambour top and
row of file drawers in flash-grain
oak, circa 1860, for the factory
manager's office. Very unusual.
$3,500.

Charming school desk with great
boot-jack cutout ends for legs, circa
1780. Good, old, brown shellac
finish.
$350.

Group of dolls in the $300-to-$400 class.

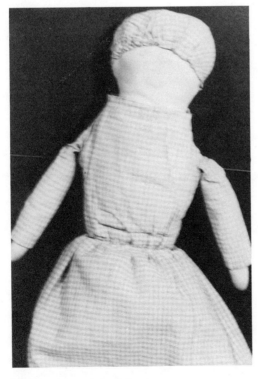

White version of Aunt Jemima topsy-turvy doll.

Aunt Jemima doll with original dress is actually a topsy-turvy doll. Pull this one's skirt up over her head and you get the white doll in the next photo. Early 1900s. Often go at auctions for over **$600.**

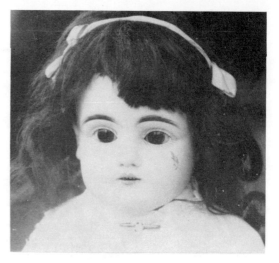

Bisque-head doll with real hair. Made in Germany for the American market in the early 1900s. Which again raises the question of what is Americana. But certainly a lot of little American girls loved them. In the area of
$350.

Aunt Jemima bottle doll. Built on a quart wine-type bottle with a sock head on the top. Early 1900s.
$150.

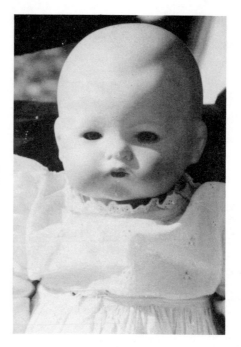

Rare baby doll made in 1880 with bisque head sewed to stuffed cloth body. They don't wet, but—
$375.

A fine bisque-head-and-shoulder doll with real human hair. Moveable eyes, fine old dress. At least **$500.**

Early bisque head just to display as an object or to make a doll around using old cloth from a ruined quilt. **$200.**

Fine French baby-faced head with moveable eyes and real hair. **$500.**

Unusual boy doll, $650. Doll on far right,
$950.

Old Teddy bears have longer arms than the current ones, and that makes them worth over
$200.

Celluloid dolls are very rare because they were so easily smashed. So this four-inch-high Babe Ruth is worth $85. (It may have been made in Japan, but anything related to Babe Ruth is still Americana!)

78

Earthenware

Large Liverpool jug, 12½ inches high, bearing the portrait of an American ship in color on one side and patriotic black transfers on other side.
$1800.

Redware pie-baking plate with dark brown splotch decorations. From mid-1800s. $150. Undecorated pie plate, right,
$75.

Pair of yellow glazed redware bowls, 17 and 21 inches wide.
$250.

Redware baked-beans jar with
handles, from the mid-1800s.
Greenish brown with dark brown
splotches. Around $150. Redware
center-hole cake mold,
  $75.

Bennington flint enameled pitcher
with the Norton 1850 mark.
  $650.

Canton rose-medallion punch bowl, 15 inches wide, brought back from China by whalers in the mid-1800s. **$1,850.**

Large Canton rose-medallion deep dish. **$325.**

Pair of Canton rose-medallion cylindrical vases with raised rosettes at top and bottom. **$825.**

Canton Mandarin spittoon from
1850s.
$750.

Canton Mandarin China brought
home by whaling fleet. The teapot,
$350. The other plates from $160 to
$250, depending on size and depth.

Fabric

Patchwork quilt from 1900. Quilts have been terribly overpromoted because they make such pretty color photos for the Sunday newspaper supplement. But they can't be washed or even dry-cleaned without soon falling apart. This quilt, **$350.**

Sewn-on pieces distinguish this very early bed cover, but design is uninteresting.
$350.

Pennsylvania-style quilts in the $600-to-$800 range.

Fine appliquéd quilt with strong
unfaded colors, made in the late
1800s. Measures 93 by 96 inches.
$475.

A geometric appliquéd and pieced
quilt in vivid colors on a pink
background.
$400.

Framed sampler with desirable heart
shape. Signed and dated.
$450.

Corner of early sampler from early
nineteenth century commemorating
the lives of two persons. Good
unfaded condition and framed.
Overall 17 by 19 inches.
$475.

Framed segment of a valance with
patriotic designs. Miss Liberty in
center. Reads "Union for Ever" on
left, "Constitution" on right.
Measures 17 by 8 inches.
$400.

Old scatter hooked rug measuring 36
by 24 inches. Done from a Currier
and Ives print.
$450.

Folk Art

Tobacconist figure, or "Wooden Indian," in original wine-red and blue paint, with tobacco leaves in left hand. Circa 1860.
$5,750.

Very old folk art figure from the early 1800s—General Andrew Jackson astride a dappled-gray horse —carved in pine. Hat, figure, horse, and tail are separate pieces of pine. Painted blue, flesh, and dappled gray. Ten inches high. $1,500 going on
$3,500.

Mason's sign found on the outside of a tavern in northern New York. Excellent primitive American art.
$2,500.

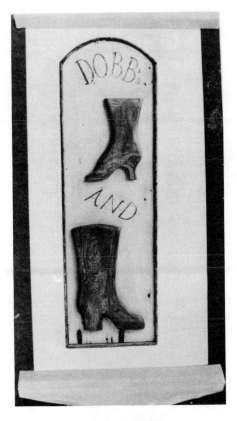

Tradesman's sign from the late 1800s. If original, $1,600. If a copy —and they often are copies—about **$250.**

Authentic hanging tavern sign with Mason's symbol dimly visible, from the late 1800s. $2,200 to one of those big-city stockbrokers.

A professional sign or carriage painter would come by your house and make a hand-lined number sign on a wooden plaque that he had already decorated. Worth now: **$110.**

Tavern sign of the early Victorian era.
$125.

Very weathered fish weather vane of great style. As weather vane, $350. As folk art in the current big-city boom, $1,200. (Stockbrokers don't buy anything priced under **$1,000.)**

Clara Cluck—here seen with some friends from other parts of this book —was a seat on a children's merry-go-round. Golden-mustard body with old greens and blue. Even though she can't find Donald, she is a real winner in the folk art department. Very heavy, made of oak blocks. Currently
$2,200.

88

Most country dealers would be lucky to get $40 for the "old checkerboard." But in a shop specializing in folk art it would go for $350 (no kidding!). For the round ditty box with initials in old paint, $250. Stiff Dutch-oven brush, **$650.**

Cigar-store Indians are usually about five feet tall. On the left, a great one with lots of character has a paint job that looks too good to be true, but is so well done that it is hard to deny that it is worth $6,500. Some go as high as $15,000. The frontiersman on the right is rarer, but people just love the Indians. Frontiersman is in the

$2,500 range.

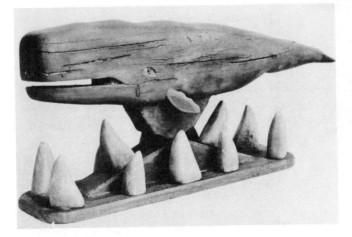

Wooden whale is not in the realistic style of other old carvings done by seamen. If the whale teeth below are real, they are worth $60 to $100. Fakes are made from old whalebone, stained and polished.

Life-sized horse's heads were used around riding stables. Made of rough-carved wood blocks surfaced with plaster of paris and then painted. This one has traces of its original mane. Worth
$800 to **$1,000.**

Top-of-a-flagpole eagle-on-ball is about as American as you can get. Usually made out of sheet metal, this one is of some hard wood, here repainted after much weathering. In metal or wood,
$1,500 to **$1,800.**

Advertising figure from the late 1800s. Stood on counter or in window of tobacco store. Plaster on metal-wire frame, painted naturalistically.
$350.

Two-foot-high top-of-flagpole eagle standing on ball is an excellent example of the kind made of sheet metal. Pieces are pounded into a mold to shape them, then soldered together. Such top quality is a good investment even at
$2,300.

Life-sized wooden bust with really well-shaped face, truly a work of art —but origin uncertain. Carved in wood, smoothed with plaster (gesso) and painted with enamel.
$1,500 to **$2,000.**

Memorial reverse painting on glass of a lady standing by her husband's tombstone.
$160.

Mortar and pestle, lignum vitae or rosewood—impossible to wear out. Perfect one, $65. If split, **$45.**

Life-sized folk art carving of woman and child. Probably carved by a slave in the early 1800s. Museum quality.
$16,000.

Hand-decorated tea box with Early American–type decoration. No, that is not a keyhole. About **$175.**

Eighteen-inch-long eagle's head that
hangs on wall. Eagles, eagles, eagles
—this one,
    $600.

Pretty good folk art chicken, 9
inches high, from the early 1900s.
Worth
    $250.

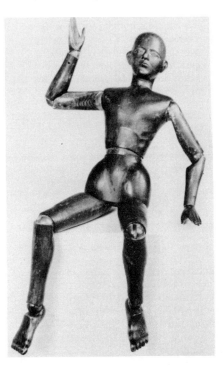

Mannekin used in drawing classes of
the 1800s.
    $350.

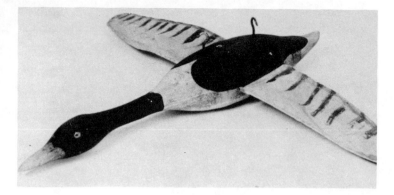

Very attractive primitive duck, about
2 feet long and in original paint.
   $350.

A wall shield or emblem of painted
wood was not unusual after 1776.
Real ones, $3,500. Good fakes,
   $700.

Eighteen-inch-high mortar with
pestle. Mortar of plaster, pestle of
wood. Used as display piece in
pharmacy in the late 1800s. Nice
paint and patina. About $350 for
this one. With a name on it,
   $450.

Marble carving about 18 inches
wide, probably from a child's grave.
Most gravestones just won't sell at
any price, but this carving is so
unusual, so artistic, that it should
bring
   $350.   94

Mustard-colored washstand from the 1830s (legs are pre-Empire). Hand stenciling with bronze powders is of the era. $350. Good, big English Stratfordshire dog,
        $225.

White chicken sign in the manner of American folk art. Not really a fake —just an imitation.
        $40.

Is this an imitation, fake, decoration? You decide. But these watermelon slices are currently going for
        $25.

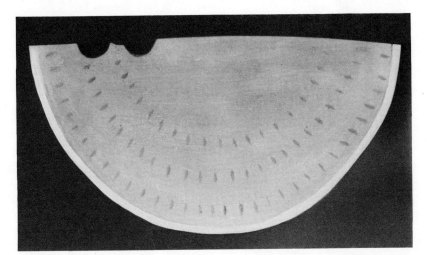

Carved and gilded eagle, 46 inches long, made for the Centennial celebration of 1876.
$1,200.

Carved carousel horses with features like these detailed glass teeth are in the
$750-to-**$1,000** range.

Hitching post for horses in the form of a black boy, from the late 1800s. Cast iron, mounted on cement pedestal, repainted, height 37 inches.
$375.

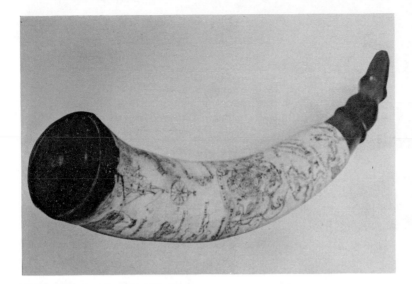

Scrimshaw case for holding maps,
circa 1776. Decorated with map of
East Coast, 13 inches long. Rare,
authentic, and
 $2,600.

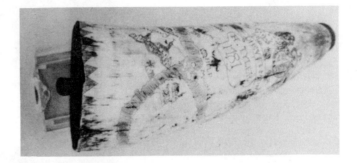

Modern scrimshaw work on old
whale tooth (soot rubbed into
scratches). Even though an obvious
fake,
 $150.

Tradesman's sign, hand-lettered by
the local carriage decorator.
 $85.

Too-good-to-be-true sign that is supposed to have hung in front of a fur trader's log cabin. Really just a kind of fantasy. Those trading outposts were rough places. As a fantasy,
        $175.

Carousel horse from the 1860s. Note front and back legs both in same position so that they wouldn't break off so easily. Fine horses from permanent merry-go-rounds go for between $3,000 and $5,000. This one was used for an itinerant merry-go-round. Even in its rough condition, this horse goes for
        $1,100.

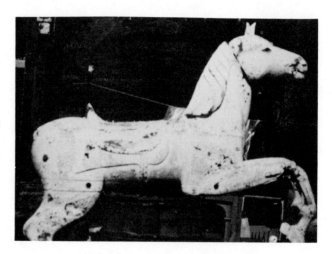

Called an "architectural ornament," this piece of painted wood probably was part of a mantelpiece in a house built in the early 1800s. The primitive painting is, of course, what's valuable. This one worth about
        $600.

From a ladies' finery store of the late
1700s, we have an almost life-sized
wood-and-polychromed half figure
for displaying dresses.
$2,500.

Well-carved, very early cigar-store
Indian. Strong face, a primitive work
of art, as opposed to later,
"decorative" Indians.
$3,200.

Buttermold of a sheaf of wheat was
pressed onto the batch of butter to
identify the month it was made.
Excellent carving,
$65.

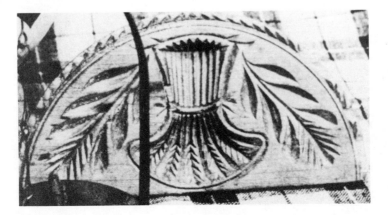

A really old carved eagle of this quality would be worth many thousands of dollars, but you would have to have proof of its age by knowing where it came from—its provenance. In the case of folk art, however, antiquity isn't the point, and the excellent job of carving makes this eagle worth
$1,200.

Good marbelized mantel made of pine, from the early 1800s. Worth from
$1,500 to **$1,800.**

Salmon sign painted in the early 1900s is easily worth
$1,200.

100

Black-boy hitching post of unusual interest, as such pieces were rarely so realistic in dress and facial expression. Although the face is something of a caricature, there seems to be as much love as prejudice in the whole piece. Controversial, but worth **$1,200.**

Ship model from the late 1800s with original canvas and knowledgeable details that would be known by an old sailor. These range from **$400** to **$600.**

Although this eagle sits on a ball, it was never used on top of a flagpole. It is just an average-quality folk art carving about 14 inches high. In the range of **$250** to **$300.**

101

Kitchen

Turned burl bowl, about 20 inches across, made from the knobby part at the base of a tree.
$100.

Maple knife box in excellent condition with turned handle.
$125.

Good early knife box from the 1830s, dovetailed with sweet curves, well-worn old paint.
$125.

Large copper and brass teapot that holds 6 quarts of water. Normal wear and dents.
$275.

Large mortar and pestle of solid brass, almost 9 inches wide. Around **$250.**

Bottle-green water bottle about 2 feet high, used for distilling grape juice in western New York State—and who knows what else in other places. At any rate, **$125.**

Large brass jam kettle, about 13 inches across. **$175.**

Bowl that Jeff Jenkins says can be used as a bowl or a scoop. Maple, soaked with vegetable oil.
$45.

Copper tank with brass knob and trim on this beautifully hand-painted ice-water dispenser from a restaurant or drugstore soda counter.
$250 to **$325.**

Routine knife-and-fork box begging for refinishing, at which point it would be worth only $45 because it is rather crude. Fine ones go up to
$125.

104

Country carrying box, probably used around the house for tools and nails. Nice old mustard paint with true patina (I'm kidding).
$65.

Wooden powder-cask with stopper missing (but easily replaced) from 1850. Red tail strapping.
$125.

Matchbox for wooden matches was hung on wall in back of stove, where matches were kept dry as well as handy. Dirty, old red paint makes it worth
$75.

Cheesebox with primitive painting on top—well, decoration. Circa 1890.
$65.

105

Candle mold with wooden frame is earlier than the all-metal ones. This one is from the middle 1700s. Made by a farmer—primitive, crude, but really authentic and Early American; so

$180.

This old-fashioned washtub was made before 1900, as the strapping is willow with rattail splicing. Pineboard sides with cedar bottom. Fine if they stay outside on the porch, but when you bring them in the house they dry out and fall apart.

$150.

Early tin chandelier with leaves on bottom. Diameter 14 inches, height 16 inches. Holds four candles. Excellent condition,
$650.

Once a fancy kerosene lamp, now converted to electricity. Circa 1900.
$120.

Slag glass lamp from the early 1900s with a Mission-and-Crafts-Movement look that is very distinctive and certainly American. This small (20 inches), simple lamp is a bargain at
$350.

Victorian-American "female beauty" ran rampant in the 1870 to 1910 era, and here we have a 12-inch figure of white metal (like pewter) on a marble base to make a lamp at the end of the Victorian era, when electricity came in.

$160.

Dietz lantern for a farmer to take to the barn, as I remember my grandfather doing. This patented design had the advantage of not bursting into flame if kicked over by a cow. You had about five seconds to pick it up—maybe more, but nobody wanted to find out.

$45.

Railroad lanterns that could either be hung on the car as running lights or be carried by the trainmen. Red, clear, and green glass. Collected by railroad buffs.

$125 each.

Right, tulip-petal lamp from the 1920s in the manner of Tiffany and Art Nouveau (using forms found in nature). $450. Glass shade in background used to hang over a dining room table in the center of room. Authentic,
$1,200.

The Three Graces, made out of powdered marble mixed with glue and cast into a mold to make a lamp base. This piece was done around 1915, as "female beauty" moved from the Victorian era to the Roaring Twenties.
$125.

Modern reproductions of very fine lampshades of the Tiffany era. These three, pieced together the same way on the original wooden molds, are $500, $750, $900. Real ones of this complexity with good colors would run
$1,500 to **$2,500.**

Nickel-plated brass Rayo (patent trade name) from the 1870s ranging in price from
$125 to **$180.**

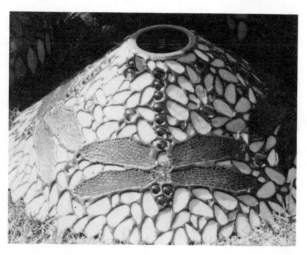

Dragonfly lampshade in the Tiffany manner of colored glass around which thin strips of soft copper have been crimped. The pieces are then soldered together on a wooden mold —exactly the same way as the originals were made. This shade for a table lamp, about 22 inches in diameter, $650. The original,
$750.

Milk-glass kerosene lamp,
$45.

110

Museum-piece early pumper for fire
department, from the 1860s. Worth
$6,000 to **$8,000.**

Flax wheel with foot pedal, circa the
1770s. Used for spinning thread.
Slow movers, so they bring only
$325.

Yarn winder of maple and pine.
Refinished,
$225.

Ship's harness cask used for storing
salted beef and pork, 30 inches high.
$1,450.

Flax hackle used for separating
strands prior to twisting thread on a
spinning wheel. Dated 1831.
$50.

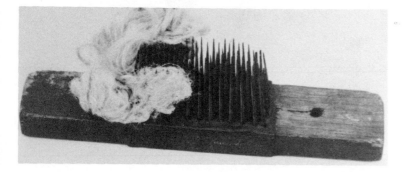

Pair of globes, one celestial, the other terrestrial, from 1816. Fine condition, 17 inches high, 12 inches wide.
$4,350.

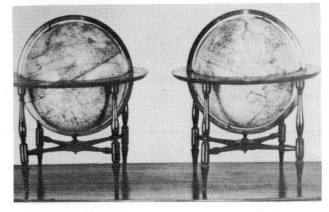

Brass chronometers mounted on double swivel joints in oak and mahogany boxes. Each around **$275.**

Wagon wheel wired to be a chandelier, $125. Unwired, **$75.**

Old stamps are a tricky business.
There are seven different printings of
this one, all with minute differences
in the scroll work. This one from the
1850s is the fifth printing—the
famous "1¢ blue." Ranging in
unused condition from
        $250 to over **$10,000.**

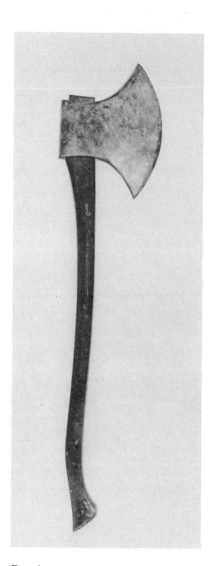

Broad ax.
$125.

Reverse side of a "1¢ blue" showing
original mucilage, an added value,
plus hinge, a deduction in value.

114

Four feet high, nice brown patina on various woods. Turnings date it back to the eighteenth century. A circular stepladder? Bleacher sets for gnomes?
$350 to **$450.**

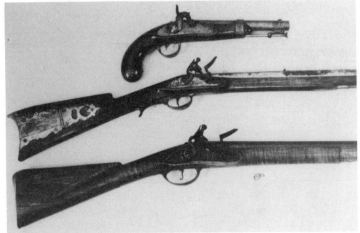

Fine percussion pistol, circa 1840, $575. Full stock Kentucky rifle, $1,450. Flintlock musket,
$750.

Collection of old wooden planes ranging from $15 to $35. Fancier ones range up to
$175.

Bedspread made on a loom, decorated with great eagles. Wool and/or cotton thread, pretty old, maybe 1850s.
$1,100.

Guns from the 1700s. Flintlocks and cap-loaded of the quality shown here (tops!) run from
$1,500 to **$2,000.**

Wooden bucket that has been hollowed out of a piece of log. Probably used on a ship.
$165. ·

Old keys are great sellers at from $1 each for these up to $5 for more ornate ones.

Excellent brass warming pan filled
with hot coal to take the chill off the
sheets. Nicely engraved, 42 inches
long, 12 across.
    $200 range.

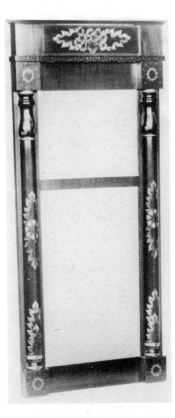

Empire mirror with Hitchcock-
chair–style stenciling on it, circa the
1880s.
    $250.

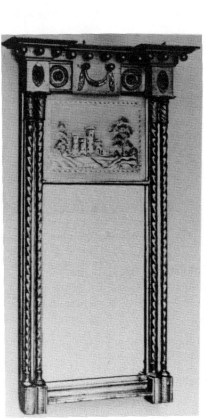

Architectural (Grecian temple)
looking glass, 40 inches high.
Reverse painting on glass on top.
Thirteen balls—the number of states
—on top. Original glass, $650. New
glass,
    $550.

Open-top cradle with original paint, circa 1800, with rockers that are sure to stop it from turning over. **$450.**

Four posts with top-end turnings, knobs on the sides to tie the baby in, in case some teenage babysitter gets too energetic. This Pennsylvania style of crib dates from the 1830s. **$575.**

Queen Anne mirror from the early 1700s. Hand-cut mahogany veneer over pine with gilded inset. A museum object. **$1,950.**

American Queen Anne mirror from the early 1700s. Mahogany veneer over pine, original silvered glass in good condition. **$850.**

118

Sailor's seabag of white cotton and blue felt stars, scrimshaw closing slide.
$550.

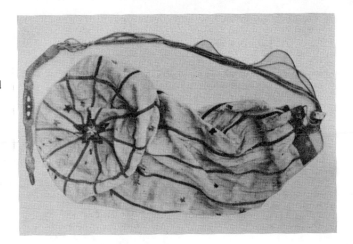

Cased brass theodolite, a surveyor's instrument for measuring angles.
$650.

Surveyor's brass compass and telescope that may have been used by George Washington.
$450.

Pewter

Pewter coffeepot with touch
signature of Rufus Dunham of
Westbrook, Maine, 1837–61. $500.
Pitcher by Thomas Boardman of
Hartford, Connecticut, 1805–50.
$600.

Pewter pieces: goblets, $650 the pair;
small plates, average $150. Large
plates (or chargers), around
$250.

Silver-plated copper teapot imitating the English.
$45.

Rare pewter coffeepot made in Massachusetts, circa 1830. Good condition, 11 inches high, $425. Brass candlesticks of same era,
$150.

Pewter mugs with fine proportions. If signed on the bottom with a metal stamp, mark of the maker, these are worth $350 or more. Unsigned, $125. Definitely a collector's item.

121

Paintings and Prints

Sophisticated paintings from American school of portraiture such as this one, unsigned, are in the **$4,500** range.

American-school portrait of a young boy from the mid-1800s was done in a busy studio, resulting in head being too small for oval canvas and body amorphous. Nice frame.
$450.

Marine paintings have a higher value when signed or artist is known. This one by Thomas Chambers, born 1808, is valued at around
$7,500.

Hudson-River-school painting 24
inches long on academy board. Blues
and grays, unsigned. Around
$250.

Pastel on paper, bright colors, by
itinerant painter of French
background. Absurd right hand and
unreal chest, but from late 1700s.
Framed and 22 inches high, so in
$600 class.

Fine American portrait in the
Gainsborough manner done by an
apprentice who emigrated to the
colony of Virginia.
$3,500.

Detail of marine painting of the kind
that runs from $3,500 to $35,000.

Watermelon paintings are always
popular. This one, by an unknown
amateur,
  $350.

An American imitation of the
French school of Corot, unsigned.
  $1,100.

Finely detailed primitive painting
reminiscent of Brueghel, unsigned.
$1,600.

1700s bad portrait of a woman,
unsigned. Not art, but as an antique,
$650.

Oysters-and-lemon still life from a
professional studio painting factory,
but nice.
$650.

Indian print of bringing home the
deer, 1910.
$225.

Well-painted farm scene, unsigned,
but still worth
$1,500.

Pair of pen-and-ink and watercolor
miniatures in bird's-eye maple
frames about 10 inches high. From
about 1830. The pair,
$400.

Pen-and-ink done by a seaman of a
steam-and-sail coastal freighter.
From 1870.
$1,100.

126

Victorian full-color print of some
children who seem to have stolen a
circus elephant and camel.
Whatever.
   $165.

Portrait of an opera singer by
unknown artist.
   $975.

Portrait of a mean old maid done by
an itinerant painter. $850—more if
she were better-looking. Honest.

127

Stern Victorian lady with big hands. Basically unsaleable but might be bought by a historical society looking for a bargain for **$350.**

Spanish-looking woman by itinerant artist. Strange bosom and the usual problem with the hands. But face is alive, so
$875.

Early portrait from the 1700s has an Early American look that is desirable. If restored, $2,500. Even before restoration for cracks and flaking (as in this picture),
$1,200.

Very realistic portrait by a good city-located portrait artist. 1790. **$1,200.**

A stylish portrait by an itinerant painter working the coast of New England in the 1840s. **$1,050.**

The size of this poor man's body, the shape of his right arm with the oversized hand hanging on it, all indicate that the body and head weren't painted by the same artist. Itinerant portrait painters often painted bodies on canvases during the winter months, when it was too hard to travel, and filled in the heads when they found a customer. In this case it looks like an assistant did the body. If this were restored, price would be $1,200. As is, $800.

Great portrait of two girls in
excellent condition.
$4,500.

Although produced by a professional
portrait studio, and in spite of the
terrible arms, the sensitivity of this
face pushes this painting up to the
$1,500 level. Restoration of the
cracked surface would cost about
$500.

Pencil drawing of husband, wife, and
daughter by the local schoolmarm or
master, done in the mid-1800s.
$450.

Three 6-by-8-inch pages from an 1890s seed catalogue. Outlines of the objects were lithographed in light gray. These were then hand-colored with watercolors with incredible accuracy. The peach, $175 framed. The other two are rare—
$225 each.

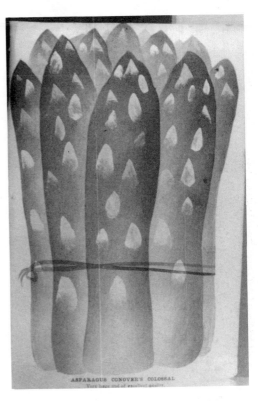

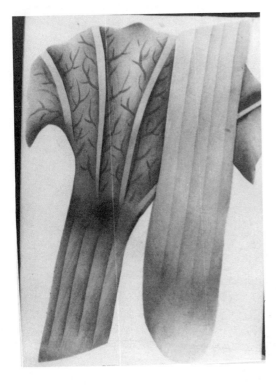

Hand-colored print from an 1850s seed catalogue carried around from farm to farm by a seed company salesman. Custom framed, $125. Nice for a kitchen wall. Unframed, $45 to $65 for these, depending on how colorful they are.

Prints of Indians were very popular in the late 1800s. Framed under glass,
$75.

Nicely done oil-on-canvas of fruit, done as an exercise in a ladies' art school. It may not be art, but it is late 1800s, so
$300.

This young naval officer or student was done by a professional portrait painter (perhaps one of the many who were itinerant) in the 1860s. Unsigned, so only
$450.

Reverse painting on glass. Attached to tombstone in the cemetery, a memorial painting.
$350.

Color print of terrific interest and popularity, circa 1900. Pasted on cheesecloth stretched on frame to simulate oil paintings on canvas, they were premiums for buying enough boxes of something. In fine condition and because of the subject,
$175.

Serious painting of a boat set in a
gilded Victorian frame.
$1,100.

Pen-and-ink drawing colored with
fading watercolors is a great
appreciation of General U. S. Grant,
so dating is obvious.
$650.

Typical seascape, circa 1900.
Unsigned, $400. If signed by known
artist,
$1,400.

Professional studio painting
(meaning the same subjects were
done over and over by one artist).
This one, 3 feet wide, is from the
1800s. Fine work.
    $1,500.

Still life of fruit from the Fall River
school, 1907.
    $350.

135

Photography

Early wooden box-camera worth about $1,100. There are special price guides devoted solely to early cameras, and your local camera store can tell you about them.

Brownie. **$5.**

Cameras of this vintage took roll film and are not particularly desired even by photographic collectors. From the 1900s. **$25.**

The collectible cameras and the ones desired as decorative objects for interior decoration are the ones like this that have a good deal of highly finished, brown, mahogany-looking wood showing in the front. These are late 1800s, and ones like this are valued at around $145. Some with lots of wood showing are twice that.

136

Traveling barber catches up with some cowboys in the 1890s. Photos showing an occupation are far more desirable than those of people or houses.
$250.

Rolling bales of cotton down the bank of the Mississippi to be loaded onto a riverboat. This photo, which is one of a series, dates from the 1890s. Such interesting photos are often found in the files of a local portrait photographer.
$350.

Kodak studio shot of a young woman, 3 by 5 inches. From the 1920s.
$25.

137

Series of four photographs for the
tourist trade from which postcards
for tourists or travelers were made.
Old prints, $150; new prints,
$35.

138

By 1915 there were 15 million automobiles on the roads and the face of America was changing—tires, too. An 8 × 10 inch print from the local photographer (or from his recently discovered files) is now worth $65. Read on . . .

The reason so many of these photographs of general interest are around is that as every town got its local photographer, he started making up postcards. Say, five a year for a thirty-year average career, times 100,000 photographers . . . This print,
   $85.

A wonderful shot of a summer rooming house in northern New Hampshire. Sort of proves that art doesn't have to be done by an artist. The spirit of a whole life and time is in this print.
   $150.

The quality of a day long past,
probably in late fall, with the leaves
that thin in the treetops . . . Who
was in those houses? Plenty of prints
like these go for
    $75.

And when he wasn't out making
postcard photos, the local
photographer was in his studio
making prints like this one which go
for only a few dollars and tell the
story of a life.

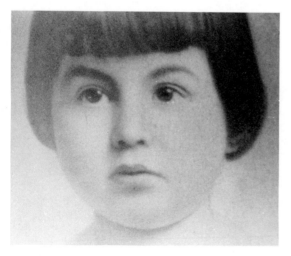

For three dollars, how can you pass
these things up? I can't.

Stoneware

Stoneware storage jar with molded handles, 17 inches tall. Usual cobalt blue decoration.
$165.

Stoneware batter jug for pouring pancakes. This piece, made in Pennsylvania, has cobalt decoration and original wooden handle. Rare, **$650.**

Two butter churns in the middle here. The one in the background, $400. The one in the foreground with original wooden pieces, $250. The bird crocks on either side, **$225.**

Unglazed Indian pottery was nevertheless refired to stabilize the painted-on decorations. About 18 inches across.
$650.

Kitchen mixing bowl, called spongeware because the decoration was put on with a sponge. In perfect condition, $325. Even with chipped edge that this one has,
$275.

Unusual two-handled water jug with great cobalt decoration. Easily
$2,500.

142

Very attractive and "artistic" unglazed piece of Indian pottery worth
$450.

Three crocks in the $200-to-$250 range. Greyhound (?) bootjack in the foreground,
$45.

Store-owned butter crock.
$275.

Rockingham-ware crock.
$75.

143

Not many lions around, so the center crock is worth $750. The two nice bird crocks, **$350** each.

Two lovebirds are super-desirable, so **$1,200.**

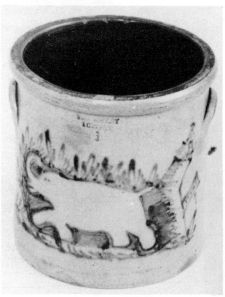

As there are probably only three elephant crocks in existence—or at least known of—the current asking price for this one is $2,500, which might make it a very good investment.

A very unusual decoration makes
this crock worth at least
$2,000.

Incisions as well as cobalt painting
on this two-handled water cooler
with hole in bottom for a spigot. But
decoration is not spectacular, so only
$750.

Crock with funny fish.
$650.

Exquisite dove on early narrow-bottomed crock. A museum-quality piece of Early American art. Currently undervalued as being just another bird. A steal at $1,200 (a "for the discriminating collector" object).

Early, narrow-bottomed, three-gallon crock.
$450.

Two birds.
$600.

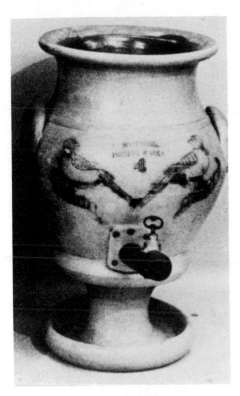

Water-cooler stoneware crock raised on a base so you can get your glass under the spigot, while the base would collect drippings.
$1,200.

A very late water cooler with hole for spigot done by an amateur "artist."
$65.

The narrow bottom indicates that this is a very early crock, but it is still the decoration that counts. This detailed bird,
$950.

147

Stoves

Cast-iron parlor stove with French lines and a classy urn on top. From the 1860s. Wide, for burning wood logs.
$750.

End-loading stove of cast iron with early curved legs in the French manner (Louis XV).
$450.

Even better similar-type front-
loading cast-iron stove of mid-1800s.
Highly desired by sophisticated
interior decorators. Especially
desirable for studio apartments or
lofts. $650. Even smaller and lower
ones that are rare,
    $850.

Toy cast-iron kitchen cookstove,
about 12 inches high, in which you
can actually light fires.
    $350.
(Yes!)

Tables

Crude, pine drop-leaf table for the poor folk in the late 1800s. Originally stained to look like dark red mahogany. As is, $135. Refinished to look like Early American brown pine,
$225.

Two-drawer cobbler's bench, circa 1800, with seven more small drawers on top is unusual, if straightforward, in its functional design. Ubiquitous because every farmer had one for repairing his children's shoes on long winter nights. This one,
$450.

A long-drawered worktable with enormous breadboard top that comes off looking much better than the one that follows. Looks more in the Shaker manner, too.
$650.

Long-drawered template table with broad working-space top. Unpopular shape, even though drawers have a Shaker look.
$175.

Scalloped corners and rope-carved legs indicate that this maple-topped table was originally stained dark mahogany in the New York City environs to pass as Sheraton from the mother country. $725 as it is, and you can do whatever you want with it.

Typically American one-drawer stand in cherry and maple with wide top, deep drawer, and Sheraton legs —the American mixture.
$375.

One-drawer maple worktable with original red paint on the base, scrubbed top, and legs in the Hepplewhite mode.
     $325.

Cherry washstand to hold pitcher and washbowl in the bedroom. Heavy-looking version of the basic Sheraton design. Circa 1840s.
     $275.

Sheraton-Empire serving table of pine with false graining and gold stripes. Circa the 1830s. Maple turned legs. All wood stained with red berry juice. Grain wiped on with sponge dipped in lampblack.
     $450.

Splay-leg workstand in cherry and maple. (Legs kept it from tipping over.)
$450.

Country-made one-drawer nightstand with tapered legs that make it float. Done in maple, circa the 1780s.
$210.

Original white paint with green trim makes this one-drawer stand very desirable. Also molding around drawer front. An investment.
$225.

153

Demi-lune serving table didn't take up much space against the wall. Figured mahogany top and maple legs. A sweet and delicate object. **$450.**

Oval-topped tap table in maple with an inch worn off the feet. Top is a replacement.
$650.

Early stretcher-based table with breadboard-type top in pine and legs in maple. Extra bold turning and original feet still intact. Original blood paint on base. Early 1700s.
$2,500.

Tavern table with wide overhang of breadboard top, deep bulbous turnings on maple legs of stretcher base, and balls on ends of feet only half worn off from rot that set in from standing on damp dirt floors of some long-ago gathering room. New England, circa 1750s.
$1,100.

154

Maple butterfly table from the 1720s with stretcher-leg frame top stained from use in a kitchen. Leaf supports resemble butterfly wings. The real thing.
$2,200.

Unusual cross stretchers on small chair table or hutch table. Lots of old paint on base, well-scrubbed pine top that was probably originally round. For the crossed stretchers,
$450.

Sheraton bedside table with leaves on both sides and two drawers is just another American mystery for
$275.

155

Breadboard-top tavern table made of curly maple. A little gem that might be worth over $2,000 if all original. But as usual, the feet and parts of the stretchers have had to be replaced due to dirt-floor rot. So, only **$650.**

Deep-leaf drop-leaf table from the virgin forests of America. These come in dark American walnut or cherry, both stained to look like Honduras mahogany. With square Hepplewhite or turned Sheraton legs. Two extra swing legs to support leaves.
$1,500 to **$2,000.**

A classic Empire rope-leg drop-leaf table made of American walnut stained to look like mahogany.
$450 to **$600.**

156

A country Hepplewhite round table with revolving lazy Susan mounted on top. Overly refinished.
$350.

Early pine washstand with primitive paint decoration done many years ago, probably in the late 1800s. For the old paint,
$350.

Country-made drop-leaf table with cherry leaves and Sheraton-style turned legs.
$460.

157

Tripod Tables

Unusual tilt-top candlestand with a birdcage mounting and a drawer inside the birdcage. Made of wavy birch.
$1,200.

Same table showing checkerboard top.

Snake-foot Queen Anne–into–Shaker tripod table for not wobbling on uneven floors and so safer for standing candles on. Late 1700s.
$650.
(Shown from bottom up.)

Maple candlestand of ugly
proportions.
$350.

American vulgarization of
Chippendale style, made around
Philadelphia of mahogany in the
early 1700s. Birdcage, dish top, ball-
and-claw feet, but not well carved
and heavy-proportioned, so only
$1,600.

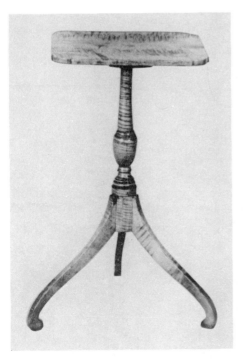

Hepplewhite candlestand with
foolish spider legs is nonetheless
made of tiger maple and has fine
Greek vase column to make up for
the legs. And the oddity factor of
the legs is also a value booster.
$1,100.

A Hepplewhite candlestand that has the twin cachet of being made of tiger maple and of having unusually bold turnings for its spider-leg design. As a result, it is in the $1,500-plus class.

A standard but very nicely made Queen Anne candlestand from the early 1700s. Classic Greek-vase column and proportions.
$1,100 range.

A clumsy Greek-vase column and heavy, stumpy legs push this Queen Anne candlestand down to the **$300-to-$400** range.

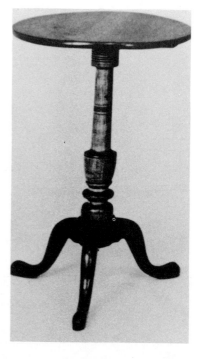

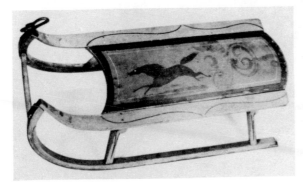

Child's wooden sled from the 1870s with good hand decorations goes for $350. "Rosebud" sleds of the Citizen Kane variety actually exist, as that was a trade name, and they go for **$1,100.**

Excellent gray rocking horse without its rockers, about $700. Cut down the middle from nose to tail to make two wall hangings, **$550** each.

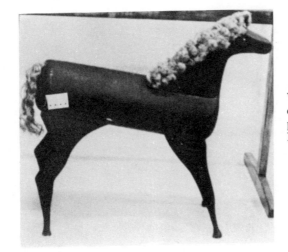

Wooden horse 18 inches high that originally stood on four-wheeled platform pulled along by a string. Nice patina. **$175.**

Rolled-steel fire truck 20 inches high
from the 1920s. Very strong toys.
$180.

Turn-of-the-century alcohol-fired
steam engine.
$150.

Tin schoolhouse of primitive origin.
$75.

162

A milk wagon to sit on and steer,
with paint in good condition.
$375.

Lead toy soldiers—French and
American allies in Revolution. Foot
soldiers, $24; officer on horse, $75.
Value depends on fineness of
decoration. These are medium grade.

British trooper on left is
comparatively rare, $125. Same for
horse with rider. Toy soldiers with
the provenance of having been
owned by various famous Founding
Fathers are worth four or five times
as much.

Block puzzles were fun. This one has lithograph-printed colored paper pasted on light, wooden four-inch-cube blocks.
$175.

Well-made clothes on early clown toy-doll makes it worth
$175.

Victorian tin boat with spring-driven motor for sailing in the park lake on Sunday afternoons, 30 inches long. Paint in excellent condition.
$1,200.

Riding horse in need of restoration.
$450.

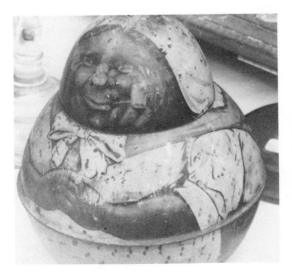

Roly-poly toy that was originally a biscuit tin. Color-lithographed tin—printed flat, then pressed into shape. This one, $550. Other characters, $400 to $650. Very collectible—meaning that some people just go crazy over them.

Super-whirligig that is a fan-driven Ferris wheel. Actually a whirligig weather vane. Early 1900s, maybe '20s.
$375.

Wood-carving toy of two oxen and harvest cart. Primitive, handmade object difficult to date.
$250.

Child's ride-in cart or wagon of the late 1800s.
$725.

166

Weathered old rocking horse with a lot of personality. Good early example despite loss of mane. Hand-carved out of pieces of pine, joined with maple dowels.
$850.

Wooden airplane with tin wing and tail, wooden propeller, $350 because of folk-art look.

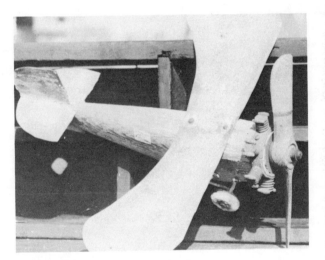

Complete Victorian rocking horse from the 1880s.
$850.

Among electric trains, the Lionel ones are the best, going for $100 to $125, even for the common boxcars. Less well-made varieties go for as low as
$25.

Victorian pool balls. For the set and rack, only $45. Seems pool players like shiny, perfectly round new balls.

Bone and ivory cribbage set brought back from China by whaling men, $175. (An object does not have to be made in America to be classed as Americana. George Washington had his uniforms made in England.)

White metal trimotor airplane with all props and wheels intact and moving freely.
$250.

Victorian slide projector of cartoon images mounted on glass slides. Light source is a built-in kerosene lamp.
$150.

Weather Vanes

Hollow copper weather vane
mounted on a custom-made iron
base, circa 1875. Perfect natural
green patina. A gem in the
$3,500 range.

Copper weather vane of galloping
horse and rider, 31 inches long.
Excellent condition.
$1,200.

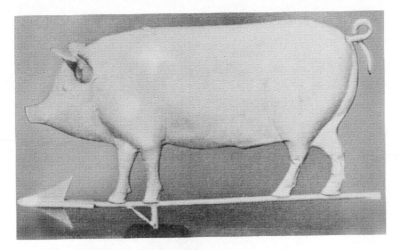

Hollow copper weather vane in the shape of a pig mounted on large directional arrow. Old mustard paint, two bullet holes.
$2,600.

Two pieces of copper sheet were hammered into matching molds, then trimmed and soldered together to make this classic running-horse weather vane. This authentic one from the 1850s has no bullet holes, as most do, so is worth $1,500. Watch out for the many recently made copies that are acid-aged and are really only worth $150 to $250. (They shoot bullet holes in the fakes, too.)

Grasshopper weather vane made of two pieces of copper soldered together. Since that is hard to do, they go for $450 with a nice green patina on the copper, or sometimes patches of gold leafing. A really old one would probably go for $25,000, if it were for sale.

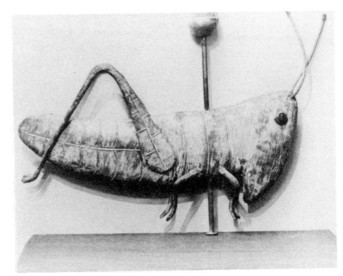

Indian archer weather vane, a painted casting of uncertain age on a real old arrow.
$850.

Early sheet-metal codfish weather vane turned out by a local blacksmith along the coast of New England.
$550.

Hundred-year-old weather vane made out of wood and painted. The value of objects like this depends on how quaint, cute, interesting, exciting, charming, or whatever they are. This one rates about
$450.

172

Classic primitive weather vane with great green patina. This really good one, $3,500. (One just like this one was recently stolen by helicopter from the top of a barn in Rhode Island a few years ago.)

Exceptionally detailed, molded, copper-sheet rooster weather vane. Remarkable.
$4,500.

Grotesquely inaccurate sheet-metal representation of a rooster from Pennsylvania. This is a $150 fake. The original sold not long ago for around $5,000. The rust was older.

A too-good-to-be-true mariner with his spyglass. Wood, painted. **$150.**

Hessian soldier whirligig made out of wood with some weathered paint still intact. Seems to be an authentic relic of the late 1700s or early 1800s. Therefore, worth **$950.**

Goose whirligig with spinning wings. Probably a pretty good fake. **$150,** anyway.

Ancient wooden trout weather vane from a barn on the edge of Lake Champlain. Nicely restored. **$1,100.**